HUNGRY MOON

The Mountain West Poetry Series
Stephanie G'Schwind & Donald Revell, series editors

We Are Starved, by Joshua Kryah
The City She Was, by Carmen Giménez Smith
Upper Level Disturbances, by Kevin Goodan
The Two Standards, by Heather Winterer
Blue Heron, by Elizabeth Robinson
Hungry Moon, by Henrietta Goodman

Henrietta Goodman

HUNGRY MOON

poems

For information about permission to reproduce
selections from this book, write to
Permissions, Center for Literary Publishing,
9105 Campus Delivery, Department of English,
Colorado State University,
Fort Collins, Colorado 80523-9105.

Printed in the United States of America.

Library of Congress Cataloging-in-Publication Data

Goodman, Henrietta
[Poems. Selections]
Hungry Moon : Poems / Henrietta Goodman.
      pages cm. -- (The Mountain West Poetry Series)
Includes bibliographical references and index.
Sixth in the Mountain West Poetry Series.
ISBN 978-1-885635-31-0 (paperback : alk. paper) --
ISBN 978-1-885635-32-7 (electronic)
   I. Title.

PS3607.O568A6 2013
811'.6--dc23

                              2013035741

The paper used in this book meets the minimum requirements of the American
National Standard for Information Sciences-Permanence of Paper for Printed
Library Materials, ANSI Z39.48-1984.

1 2 3 4 5   17 16 15 14 13

for my mother,
and for my sons, Cole and Scott,
again and always

CONTENTS

PART I

HUNGRY MOON

*Part of the total fantasy of greed is always
the attempt to eat up one's own appetite.*
—Adam Phillips

Driving home I tell my son the moon is full
and he says *no, hungry moon* because he is two

and wants dinner and sees how the moon follows
our car across the bridge, bobbing unpoppable

above powerlines, the splintery tops of phone poles,
in a sky black and frictionless. Passing over it now,

a little lasso of gray cloud catches, then drifts,
no longer backlit, no longer an empty ring. A string.

If the moon is greedy, then what it wants is to collapse
in on itself—to fly shrinking, shrieking out of orbit.

But if it's hungry, it can wait—footprints frozen
in lunar dust, some piles of human junk. If greed

is the desire to end hunger once and for all
then greed is a death-wich we eat until we're gone.

Lab rats live longer if they never get enough.
Hunger brings long life, says the fortune cookie

broken open and left on the table. What we need
is a hunger that feeds on what it eats, the way I watch

my love rack the balls, chalk the cue, then set down
the blue cube like an empty glass, with a deliberate

thump. I'll never stop. Years ago, I stood on the scale
at 88 pounds, calculating, bloodless, obsessed. I've hardly

mentioned it since. But even then I was too sane to starve,
learning to leave hungry only in order to return.

DOG WITH STICK OF DYNAMITE

It's like a cartoon, the way he runs around us wagging
his tail, part collie, part mystery, his face a double mask
of comedy and tragedy. Ears up in sharp points and he's a wolf
with eyes like insects caught in amber—soulless, stalled
in history. This is the dog who turned from the trash can
on Christmas Eve, snarling and snapping like a tangle of wire
rolling off a spool, pinned my son to the kitchen floor
with the paws I had called *dainty,* and tore a two-inch flap
of skin from his skull, ripped his cheek as though it had split
from its own chubbiness, red stuffing spilling out.

This is the dog we rescued, fed, who could fold his ears
down into soft little envelopes, who let me shampoo
his matted fur in the yard with the hose in cold October—
grateful, sharp-ribbed and pale-tongued. Long gone,
he returns, tossing his head, the red stick in his mouth
spitting sparks. We yell *Rhodes, Rhodes, drop it, go away,*
and he thinks we are playing—the thing in his mouth,
clenched between his teeth, who to blame? He is the same—
the harm both him and not-him—*Rhodes,* we say,
Rhodes, spit it out, but he never can.

AFTER BIRTH

I was trying to type *encyclopedia* but kept typing *envy*
when I got to the part where my son
sprawled on the bed, asking *what's a placenta?*
So we went to the *envy envy* encyclopedia,
so helpfully literal, so unopen to interpretation.
I remembered my own, or his, sliding out
numbly, how a nurse caught it in a bowl
and was going to take it away, but I strained
to sit up, to look. Building a placenta is hard work
the body does without the mind—temporary organ,
bound by the scope of its own necessity.
It was yucky, I tell my son, sticking out my tongue.
How big? he asks, and I say it was like a black brain—
an anti-brain, lumpy pillow with a white
amniotic fringe—

painless, painless, that predictable end.

AURORA

The mother cuts two holes in the white sheet. Her hands
are ice, the child a ghost now except her feet, her hands.

Lambs for graves of children, sheep for mothers.
Too tired to sleep, she stares as years concrete her hands.

In April, the lake is an egg, a sugar skull.
Black water rises up through ice to meet her hands.

Green sheets of light billow on a skyline of *what
they want to see*—she knows the night will cheat her hands.

How well they remember what they didn't see: blind
eclipse of Nefertiti's eye, the heat, her hands.

She said *can I,* he said *will you,* and she did,
and does, and would, but still the rings defeat her hands.

Still he calls her by the name her mother used
when she was good, still his hands complete her hands.

FLY OR CRAWL

In the beginning, all small things
that fly or crawl are bees,
and then the insect-whole
fragments into butterfly, spider—
first generalized, then categorized
by sting. The undivided self
is not a self but a zygote.
All other divisions follow.
My son asks what would happen
if we sliced a bumblebee in two.
On the radio Gwen Stefani sings
I ain't no Hollaback Girl,
and my son sings *There ain't no
Hall of Ector. Is that it?* I ask.
He pauses, thinks, begins again—
There ain't no Holy Vector—

WITCHWATER

Witchwater shimmers black as liquid tar,
and you think it's a mirage, an innocuous trick of physics,
but drive over it and your tires will stick. You weigh
more here, and the air you swim through smells like a woman
you'd leave before she wakes up older than last night,
toys scattered over the sticky floor and a half-eaten sandwich
drying out on a Corelle plate—

Despite the bridges, the buildings that float
over the distant city like steel lily pads, you're under water
here, the night stuck on pause at that point where everything's
black and white as an old TV show—the whole family
eating canned corned beef hash, grown-ups watching whatever's on,
children sprawled transfixed on the itchy carpet.
You might not notice at first, that the tar of the road
you're trying to leave on covers the bones
of saber-toothed tigers.

OUTSIDE THE VIDEO STORE

Outside the video store, a man in fingerless gloves
sits on a three-legged stool playing a cello—the bow
sawing as though to sever the strings, then dancing
alone in a slow sarabande as I walk to my car,
snow melting as it touches asphalt, the handle
of my plastic bag denting the crook of my arm.
The notes stretch thinner and thinner, past two men
propped against the brick wall with cans of beer,
past people idling in the handicapped spot to drop
movies in the night return, until this public sadness
engulfs each private pain like oily rivulets draining
through sewer grates—the case open, red lining
exposed like a body split down the middle, rain-pocked,
sun-lightened, slicked by the oil of coins and hands.

THE PATH TO IMMORTALITY

Voices rise three floors from the street, thrown by wind.
Everything we do has been done by wind.

Ice strikes the window like sand. In his sleep he asks
for a ride to a place only known by wind.

Which shore does Zhao Bing look toward as he floats
over the river on a woven mat, blown by wind?

In a winter field, a boy waits while his father photographs
the moon obscured by clouds, shown by wind.

A pheasant crows in the frozen furrows. Dry stalks
crack under his feet, last year's seeds sown by wind.

Someone says *I told you not to touch me,* says *please
I want to go home*—to be left alone by wind.

I wrap my legs around his legs, my hands around
the bars of the bed. We're carved, like stone, by wind.

WHERE SADNESS COMES FROM

Your father hunting pheasant in the fields
behind the house, you and your brother
waving sticks in your hands, one of the barn cats
pouncing on mice in the stubbled furrows
like swells of a frozen ocean—

your father hunting grouse in the Wisconsin
woods, you and your brother old enough
for guns slung over your shoulders as you pass
between a cliff stratified like a book
and a creek so full and fast its echo throbs,
a machine in the rock—

you and your brother like wind in a stand
of leafless birch, surprised how little force
it takes to push the trunks over, how tall
they are—twenty feet, thirty—

and the sound of their crashing—rootless,
overlapping, white poles with blank scrolls
of bark, black knots of missing branches.

CANADA

When he rows out to collect the geese,
they see him floating like an unexpected god,
oval hull weathered gray, oars treading
the dark water. They see him coming,
a boy barely more than retriever
of wing-shot bodies, see how he snatches them
from the scum of ice and wrings them
like he's turning the crank of a machine,
so hard sometimes the neck snaps,
then winds to a thread, then severs,
body flung back into the water, head
and black beak dripping in his hand.

When he rows out to collect the geese,
he thinks, like any god, this is just
what you do. They see him coming and dive
if they can, and swim, stroking in slow
motion, water rolling over their wings—
and him in the boat, and them knowing
he'll catch them and him knowing they know—

CLAY PIGEONS

Even after a man yells *pull* and the mesh door
of the cage flaps open, they squat immobile,
dull gray and sculpted in the suburban mist,
their signal to flush more private than this place—
three miles past the skeet range, doctors
in Filson coats drinking cans of beer
and peeling hundreds off a roll. To win,
they drop the bird in a circle chalked
on the ground. Always, here, you're a boy
among men, feathers warm through your gloves,
each hole a bead of blood. Always the men
shooting, talking, the words just widening
clouds of breath, and you outside the ring,
reserving judgment, waiting for a sign.

PART II

FIRST FLIGHT

Eyes closed you rise over frozen American Falls,
the cold motel, the Quik Stop's fridge full of sandwiches
and small bottles of livestock vaccines,
the mortuary's neon rose—
When you look below, it's all white ice,

the reservoir marbled and swirled like burlwood,
where air, or land, is trapped—
no sound but the pure noise of the engine,
the gas needle broken, shuddering
at the bottom of the gauge.

A flock of white birds turns all at once
against gray sky, and their shadows turn on ice.
The Idaho plain breaks into hills, then mountains
pushed up from beneath, swollen to bursting—
trees black against snow.

When the plane begins to pitch, you understand
only half of turbulence, imagine each patch of trees
a black hole, the thinner air easier to fall through,
as though darkness could exert a pull,
become a swirling pool that wants you in it.

But each time after this, it's the updraft from the black
that lifts you up, arms crossed, fingers clutching
your ribs, the plane a bird riding a thermal—
and the empty snow you cross back over
that jolts you weightless, into freefall.

NAVIGATION

The ridge, burnt black, too steep for trees,
drops away and we descend between canyon walls,

our plane a chip of flint in the white sky, the strip
a mown X still strewn with winter's bones,

stall horn sounding as our wheels touch the grass.
Sailors fed a knotted rope through their hands

to judge speed, kept the compass in a wooden box,
suspicious of whatever spirit steered the collisions

of current and wind. At night they dreamed
of love and murder—skin hot and dry in sleep,

delirious as sea-water-drinkers. Of course
we are guided by forces we don't understand—

choice plays no part. And what of trust?
At night they closed the lid, locked the trembling

needle in like an animal, like a dead thing,
as though that could possibly help.

THE WIND I MEAN

There are knobs he turns and knobs he pulls
and knobs he pushes and knobs he turns slowly
and knobs he turns quickly, a knob that changes
the speed of the propeller and a metal bar
on the floor he raises or lowers and something else
that feels like the plane is stopping, like we are not
so much flying as floating—
bobber on a line, tugged by current,

as though what's controlling us is above us,
not him in the seat beside me, one hand
on my knee, the other on the yoke,
not him rolling a cigarette, tapping ash
out the window, Sonic Youth on the headsets—

as though this is a secret
we both know but can't share—

I could call it crosswind, the rear of the plane
swishing like the tail of a fish, or the tailwind
that makes us fast, the headwind like a wall,
the shudder of carburetor ice, or just mild turbulence,
not even the kind that could shake us like a ball
attached to a paddle by elastic string, fling us
against the roof, the walls, if we weren't buckled in—
but it isn't the wind I mean.

AIRBORNE

I said if the end of the world is coming, let it
come now, so we can go together—then threw up
into a plastic bag from bad calamari. So much
unexpected pleasure—that rooftop restaurant,
sun and cold beer after seven months of sky
like cold cement, that string of lights, each bulb
cased in a ruby teardrop, froth of green in the tops
of trees, our specific unguarded presence—
these particulars his theory ignores. To have
a plane and fly it, to land gently on a grass strip
between two burning brush piles, the Swan River
rushing down its mossy flume to the dam. Those lost
seagulls. A red kayak running the rapids. The hat
he wore. All the while insisting it's not the person
but the feeling—roving, airborne as a disease, a spore.

WILLFUL BLINDNESS

So you know what it's really like: Cindy almost blind,
her daughters twin shapes on the grass. When a bee
stings one, both scream. Her fingers wade
through their tears, feeling for the welt, the stinger.
In a flurry of blossoms, hummingbirds dive for sugar
from a giant plastic berry. I'm tired of seeing
how tired of seeing you are, tired of good advice
misapplied: stay by the wreckage, drain gas
from the wings of the plane for fire and wait.
Look for help and you end up stripping naked
by a frozen stream and lying down in snow. I know
a business that will turn the ashes of loved ones
into beautiful jewelry. That's all I want now,
the only ring I want to put on.

FAIRY SLIPPER

Beware the frozen Ides of March. Beware
the self-betrayal of a little knowledge poorly
applied. Next time he rolls toward you in the hour
before dawn, you will say yes no matter what
he has or hasn't done. You will listen to gesture,
not word. Not the fairy slipper, but the way it unfurls
like a squid, the gray fur at its heart. You would take
any flower now, even the drunken flower of his breath,
the exhaust atomized, damp and oily in his clothes.
Even the flower of his waiting while you pour
a thermos of coffee. Even to read the forecast
with him, to see in the string of letters and numbers
BR, which is mist, to hear him say in your ear
Baby Rain, flower of recognition, under snow.

GROUND EFFECT

When the bruise turns yellow you want him
to see how hard he pushed you away. It's natural
to flinch if anything comes too close, not evolutionary
to pause, to ask the hand what it plans to do.
In the Hot Springs pool, nearness was necessity,
not choice. You could have touched him. You could have
touched anyone—the woman sitting in a black coat
on the concrete edge soaking her feet, the boy
on his knees humming, eyes closed, in the steam.
In the plane, your hair still damp and smelling of sulfur,
silver bracelet tarnished blue-green, he rattled down
the rutted asphalt strip, hovered for ground effect,
then rose straight up, the valley a lake of clouds,
nothing but the Mission Range and wilderness
beyond, snow and rock, mountains replicating like cells,
avalanche trails branching like winter trees, the veins
of a hand, like all the blood of the body running away
from the heart. Below the plane, waterfalls, whirlpools
of cloud, above, undifferentiated blue. The boy in the pool
tilted his face like a plant to the winter sun, a trench
up his stomach, deep pocks in the flesh like alien navels.
If you had to land, you could not land.

TWO ON THE GROUND

Along the road, a flutter like winter-black
leaves, inner-tube rubber. I stop the car,
and it's birds locked together, one pinned
to the snow, wings beating, flapping like bats,
the way film sped up obliterates grace.
Then separate, graceful again, they swoop
to the gutter of a trailer. In a series
of still shots, disintegration is instant,
the chair whole, the chair broken, none
of the wobbling, the squeaking, the child
kicking his heels, tilting back on two legs,
standing on the rungs. We talk about people
this way, whole and broken. That's not how it is,
no matter how it looks—two on the ground,
one hovering over the other.

QUISCALUS MEXICANUS
(GREAT-TAILED GRACKLE)

> *. . . these vagabond troopers, so common everywhere*
> *as to come under the contempt of familiarity.*
> —*The Coues Check List of North American Birds,* 1882

Familiarity is not our problem. Our problem
is the birds in the tree next door—all winter,
squawking deep in the only green.
By April, so loud I can barely hear you.
On the ground they wobble, tails cocked
like skewed keels, the sheen of their feathers like oil
on wet asphalt. White-eyed, their sockets look pecked clean.
At dusk, at dawn, they shriek the soundtrack
to the shower scene in *Psycho,* violins
composed to screech like grackles, like a knife
ripping flesh: *rank-rank-rank-rank,*
reek-reek-reek-reek-reek, the sound you make
when you mean to say a woman's crazy.
If you could hear me, I'd say it's a woman
being murdered. You'd say *too dumb*
to lock the door. I'd say *don't go.*
You'd say *lock the door.* Even now,
ornithologists disagree over what Linnaeus meant
by *Quiscalus*—maybe an onomatopoietikon,
maybe early Portuguese for *quail,* or maybe
from the Spanish *quisquilla: a trifling dispute, a triviality,*
or the Latin *quisquiliae* for *refuse, dregs,*
the small twigs and leaves which fall from trees.
So the birds are fighting over nothing,
as we do. Or the Latin *quis* for *who.*
We hear it all day and all night, that stabbing arm
raised, a whirlpool of blood down the drain,
reek-reek-reek-reek—
and even now, I hardly know you.
Who is crazy? Who to blame? Quis?

EMBARKING

That Saturday you carved pineapple boats,
remember, the dog lapping bacon grease,
the slow Morse code of pigeons' minor notes?
I saw how far we'd come from simple peace,

our early faces guileless, less disguised.
Not slow enough, this meal, or no matter
how slow, it ends in empty boats capsized
on sticky plates, bowls crusted with batter:

we make it, so we can make it over.
But even as you hollowed out each hull
beneath a tough strip of core to cover
the sweet triangular rowers who sculled

themselves into our mouths, I wanted more—
our first embarking, the moment before.

AFTER FIGHTING WE FLY

Why did I have to get above it to love it—
the flatness of this earth, cotton fields,
oil wells lit up like gallows, towns unbound
by the margins of valley, amoeba-shaped
spills of light spreading, linked by dark roads
on which a single car creeps, headlights
blurred to one? From the ground,
I never saw how these constellations—
Tahoka, Lamesa, Odessa—mirror
the clusters of stars coming out now
in blue-white, gold, pale green.
I never saw this flock of red-lit windmills
flicker like a distant fire, like the pulse
of hundreds of heart monitors,
a field of poppies grown bright on bone
and blood. Past these banks, the low
red glow of civil twilight fades to civil dusk,
then nautical, astronomical twilight—
the stars above, the stars below
and us between.

PART III

IN A CLEARING

Disturbed, the snow crust talks—
all tooth, and tooth underneath.
The brain talks to the fingers

and toes in a clearing
white as a rolled-back eye
and then is silent. A blister

of ice over water seeps.
We sit on two rocks, my foot
pressed against his chest

in a warmth that is not personal.
All that time I drifted like snow,
toward whatever would stop me.

MAGNETITE

Who wants to admit it's mostly heat
we're after, blind and blameless
as missiles? It's nothing special
to be a body bending toward another
body like a plant toward light,
to be dumb as butterflies magnetized,
overlapping on a filigreed leaf—
to be ruled like that, pinned
from the beginning.

DESTRUDO

We stopped on the bridge to watch
the rush of spring runoff divide
around pilings, blue as a vein.
Like psychic vertigo, that sense
that the mind might suddenly split,
and one half push the other out
over the water—the body drawn down
by the force of fear and unwished
temptation, the railing so low,
even the wind could do it. I stood
in your arms, your chin on my shoulder,
the sky perfectly ripe. Behind us,
the red sun teetered like a car
on the edge of a cliff, then dropped.
I forgive you for saying you'd catch me—
I would've said it too.

WHAT LETS YOU WIN

Tonight your calm is all potential fist.
He wants to make you hit him first, but when
beer soaks your shirt, you shoot and two balls kiss
then drift. You've got his wife. What lets you win

is slop, not plan, but who can tell? Someone
yells *I was robbed* and drops a cue, but you
just want to drink enough to sleep. No fun
to fight with him, and you're no thief. But who

can tell? Outside, the November sky spits
white buckshot in your face. It's not too late
to change your mind, but you're the wedge that splits
by depth, by force, and not by choice. You'd wait,

except in this you're just a tool, a thing.
She takes off her dress, she takes off her ring.

OBJECT LESSON

I had back all I'd lost, and thought,
this time, to keep it—the small room,
the noon heat, tubes of paint squeezed
onto newsprint. In Lafreniere Park
white birds stood in the black water
for hours in the same pose, needle-thin
and hungry. I held out my sugar-covered
palm, offered bits of beignet to the swan
who swam near and burbled softly.
In my red dress I sat in that picture
he sketched and discarded until
perspective was everything—
the swan a cobra, rising.

PARTING GIFTS

The gift he gave the last time we parted—
a blue-green lozenge of Venetian glass
I clutched all the way across Texas
to that hotel at the edge of some town
I drove up to and stopped—in the bathroom
a clear box mounted to the wall and a note
in blue pen, *please dispose of needles
safely*—his phone ringing in my ear as I waited
in my clothes on the gritty sheets,
men's voices outside, sirens and thunder.
It held us up a long time, that story.

FIRE SEASON

A red bucket hangs from the helicopter
like the closed bloom of a tulip,
then opens to spill a portion of the lake
on the smoke at the top of the ridge.
What we are doing is not similar enough.
We sit on the pebbled shore, my arms
looped around his chest the way I'd hold
a child without a seatbelt in a speeding car,
my fingers filling the shallow gaps
between his ribs. Soon, he'll disappear
into the story he's telling, the jaundiced
dusk. In the lake, minnows weave
through my legs like cats, slim
as splinters. They kiss my ankles,
the red polish on my toes, the brush
of their mouths soft but persistent,
like they want inside.

HELL: DETAIL OF A COUPLE IN BED

What he tells her, finally, is that demolition
sucks—the dirty joke he didn't get for months,
his arm numb from swinging a hammer.
They talk by lamplight until the mantle
collapses like spun sugar. So much
to dismantle: his innocence, hers, the fruit
of their losses. It's not what he did,
but that he can't confess. She'd be his
confidante once more, then never—
and still, they can reach across
this little crevasse.

He thinks he's writing it down in ink,
but it's ice, hoarfrost rising like magnetized
filings over what really happened
until a new story sets in like a hard freeze.

He's already left out *the blood
on her white dress,* added *a fox in the snow.
She makes her fingers into quotes,
or, she makes the shadow of two
antelope on the wall.*

MATRYOSHKA

She orders a Black Russian. If you were paying
attention, you'd know what this means—
she's across the table, nodding, smiling,
but a woman inside her is thinking of a man
in overalls, a potato farmer, maybe,
a Black Sheep Potato Farmer who reads
Dostoyevsky and plays *can I will you* in bed.
All along you've been an inept spy, mistaking
poems for letters, letters for poems, caring
more about first person than third. In the car
she turns the radio up until a small electric
shock starts mid-spine and rises like a bubble
of serious laughter, like the chill of epidural
anesthetic, until the top of her head
feels like it's coming off. Don't be sad
when she's gone—it has more to do
with Emily Dickinson than with you.

PENELOPE AT THE WHEEL

A young man walks toward the jukebox and I follow him because
I'm tired of listening to the old man with a pocket of chew in his
bottom lip slur his way through the same question again and again.
Out the window, the water tower floats, a bloated fish ringed with
red light. When we met after a year apart, he brushed his hand
over my palm, across the callus at the base of each finger, then held
an ice cube, let it melt where he drew it down between my breasts.
In the morning, gone again. It was good to have something to wait
for, to write those careful letters—if not beautiful then terrible
told well. But the other thing, the thing I tore apart each day, only
a fool would do it—each night the wasted passion of a one-night
stand, bored and objectless. Someone takes a picture and the flash
explodes against my face with the force of a slap. One day I'll end
up in a box with those black and white photos of men on a wolf
hunt, nameless children unsure whether they're allowed to smile.

SPRING WEDDING

Oregon, again—orchards of sagebrush
and then the lush valley, the floating snow
of Mt. Hood. Red poppies flare by the sides
of the road despite how anyone feels,
and instead of grass, a carpet of emerald
leaves and tiny white petals like grains of rice.
If I fill my arms with flowers and wait
on the cliffs above the river, who knows
what sorrow might decide it no longer
owns me and rise to give me away.

A DOZEN ROSES

10:45 on a Wednesday morning, I'm driving down Texas Avenue
past a warehouse curb lined with broken chairs
and a washing machine, its eraser-colored hoses
severed like the vessels of a heart abandoned
halfway through a transplant,

when I have to stop for a man in a dirty T-shirt crossing the street
with a bouquet of at least a dozen roses, holding them
in both hands like a sword, a swaddled baby, a glass
he's trying not to spill. A black dog trots behind him,
leash dragging on the asphalt.

It's like passing a wreck, the way I want both to avert my eyes
and to follow him down the cracked sidewalk
into whatever yard of stunted crabgrass, his shoulders
hunched, expression unreadable under the brim
of his cap, the roses wrapped in clear plastic—

I want so badly what he is walking toward
to be something good.

PART IV

TELLING IT

When you find out, you want to tell and tell, but you don't know the whole story, and you never will. At seventeen, an amoeba of insecurity and ego, you floated in his car through West Virginia, past mining towns, shotgun houses lit up for Friday night. He drank from a six-pack on the floor and sang: *I was a kamikaze pilot, they gave me a plane, I couldn't fly it.* At 3 AM, you stumbled out into the fog, the only two people awake in the world. He stood behind you, turned you to face the full moon, circled by a pink ring—inside him already what will happen spinning like a maple seed, wings only good for falling.

You got back in the car and drove on, and when you find out it's years too late. He said what you did wasn't done until you told it, when you went somewhere you weren't there until you told it. The problem now is still what it was then—he can't tell you, you can't tell him.

WHAT YOU DON'T KNOW

What you don't know is your own fault. Any minute,
you'll take one more step and stumble, caught in a snarl

of barbed wire and poison ivy, and he'll put his hand

on your shoulder. Ask him a goddamn question now,
because three years from now when he puts a gun

in his mouth, what you don't know will be your problem.

Six stories of black windows rise above the hole
in the fence, and you're going to take him in, if you can,

past the elevator shaft, the stuck machines, all the way

to the wavering roof, its view of the empty water tower,
one rusted panel kicked in like a door. But now

he's stopping behind you, almost on your heels,

saying *easy* the way he'd try to calm a horse, or the racing
heart of one of the engines he tears apart. For all

his gentleness as he kneels to untangle you strand

by strand, you might as well be an engine. You just
stand there, trembling under his hands.

SEVENTEEN

No matter how you long to feel them melt
on your tongue, the white petals falling
in the dog days of August will never turn
to snow. This is one of the things
you wanted to tell him, that he had shown you
how to see this impossible blossoming.

But he had his own flat earth, his own
blindness. At five, bouncing in a dune buggy
full of spilled beer and cheap binoculars,
he had wondered—if men crawled
across the face of the moon like ants
on a slice of white bread, why couldn't he
see them? Years later, a man propped
against the post office wall with a can
of beer said *boy, you got awfully hard eyes.*

No matter how many of his stories
you recorded in your notebook,
thinking you were solving a puzzle—
who he was, what had made him
who he was—you hardly had
to know him. What you loved
was your own face turned to the sky,
your own mouth open.

NOT FALLING, NOT FALLEN

Why can't the snow just be pretty,
floating aimlessly in the winter sun?
The way it drifts reminds you
of lint, not flakes but filament,
fuzzy detritus of some infinite shroud.

You used to tell him you'd made
your own religion, stitched it
like the girls who sat through lectures
with knitting needles and balls of yarn.
It was unfinished, imperfect—
he didn't have to believe in it, exactly—

but you wanted to give him that
fabric not ever through losing
threads of itself, not torn, not whole,
not pure or not-pure, not falling,
not fallen, not exactly.

HUNGER

What did he think as he led you
down the dark hall, covered you
with his blanket, put your purse
on a chair? You woke alone
in your clothes, his double bass
on a stand at the foot of the bed
in winter sun, pear-shaped,
a voluptuous dressmaker's dummy.
You imagined his hands on the fat strings—
grease under the nails, a blister
in the web where thumb met palm.

All that time you wanted to live on air
like a plant, stretched taut, thin as paint
on the walls, to make no noise,
no awful thumping—
weren't you hungry, you stupid girl?
You said no before he asked.

ELEGY FOR THE LAST TIME

And now he is nothing but long hair falling raggedly
down to the middle of his back, the dark brown
of black coffee, lighter near the ends. Home
for Christmas almost twenty years ago,
I stepped up behind him in the Milestone Club,
drowned in the throb of bass, the floor shaking,
and lifted his hair in my hand. Its warm weight
spilled through my fingers. I gathered it
in my fist for just a moment, let it go,
embarrassed, when he turned—

veiled, now, at the moment of turning
and something immeasurable, even then,
in the unropelike length of his hair,
not braided, not even stuck together
by static, the end of each strand
so far from where it started.

THIS IS HOW YOU CAN TELL

If a girl ever drives three hours alone to a bar where she's too
young to buy beer,

if she stands in the back in red lipstick watching the black,
hammer-struck moon of your thumb as you play guitar,

if she follows you home along a two-lane road over dead
snakes and possum, past kudzu-covered trees rearing up
through the fog,

if you pull over where the road splits and she pulls over behind
you and you sit in her car drinking coffee from a thermos while
Muddy Waters sings *I'm a man, a full grown man,*

if you thump the side of her car twice with the palm of your
hand before you go, a band of bluish light already spreading in
the sky behind you—

she loves you, I promise, even though she hasn't said so.

SOLUTION

The sign along the road that says *Thickly Settled*
means population, not soil,
but how many years ago did the horse
begin to cross the ice? I wade out,
the lake bottom hard-packed beneath an inch
of sediment inlaid with some globular weed,
the horse's spiked ribs still tethered somewhere
in the dark water like an ultrasound image—
my son's ribcage floating ghostly
in a black sphere, just large enough
to hold a tiny bird. Above the lake,
sun streams through bars of cirrus.
When my friend said the aftermath
of grief was solution, he meant science,
not remedy: the way grief drags us down
like a load of snow-covered logs,
then begins to lift, the way my feet
cloud the water.

THERMODYNAMIC ELEGY

I step off the trail for a packtrain to pass and everything
hums: electric wires strung overhead on androgynous

steel towers, flies sizzling on the droppings of horses.
Snakes of smoke rise from the parched basket of Hell's

Canyon, and the creek descends in a white rush that makes
its own wind, stalls in a dark pool where clots of algae

bloom, then pours through the dam in combed rows. A wall
goes up when I think too far into it, the way someone chased

in a movie runs into a blind alley, the way the earth spins
dizzily if you lie still and close your eyes. Lie still

and close your eyes, wherever you are, and I won't try
to imagine what it's like. Where the trail crosses a rockslide,

a sudden coolness rises between rocks. I pick one up,
hold my hand over the black draft, then put it back.

ACKNOWLEDGEMENTS

I would like to thank the editors of the following journals, in which some of these poems first appeared, sometimes in slightly different forms:

Basalt: "Thermodynamic Elegy," "Ground Effect," "First Flight"
Cimarron Review: "After Birth"
Cutthroat: "Two on the Ground"
Field: "Willful Blindness"
Guernica: "Canada"
The *Massachusetts Review:* "Hungry Moon"
Memoir (and): "This Is How You Can Tell"
Mudfish: "Dog with Stick of Dynamite"
NEO: "Fire Season," "Matryoshka," "What Lets You Win"
New England Review: "*Quiscalus mexicanus*"
New Orleans Review: "*Hell: Detail of a Couple in Bed*"
Talking River: "Airborne," "Solution," "In a Clearing"
Valparaiso Poetry Review: "Navigation"
White Whale Review: "Destrudo," "Magnetite"

"Clay Pigeons," "Where Sadness Comes From," and "The Wind I Mean" were awarded a Dorothy Sargent Rosenberg Poetry Prize in 2009, for which I am grateful.

I would like to thank all of the poets who participated in my writing group in Missoula for their insight, inspiration, and companionship: Ryan Benedetti, Danny DiMezza, Violet Hopkins, Keetje Kuipers, Robert Lee, Deborah Morey, Natalie Peeterse, Sarah Weatherby, and especially Luc Phinney for taking the group into cyberspace.

I wrote or revised many of the poems in this book while working toward my PhD in English at Texas Tech University. I would like to thank my dissertation committee, Jacqueline Kolosov, William Wenthe, and Curtis Bauer, and I would also like to thank Texas Tech for its support in awarding me a Provost's Fellowship for Doctoral Studies in Creative Writing and an AT&T Chancellor's

Fellowship. I am also grateful to the Mountain West Poetry Series, and especially to Stephanie G'Schwind, for making the publication of this book possible.

Thank you to Pete O'Connell for making me fly.

The poems in part IV of this book are in memory of Kevin McKechnie.

This book is set in Sabon
by the Center for Literary Publishing
at Colorado State University.
Copyediting by Kristin George Bagdanov.
Proofreading by Mary Ballard.
Book design and typesetting by Kaelyn Riley.
Cover design by Ben Findlay.
Printing by BookMobile.